Applying the Standards: Evidence-Based Writing
Grade 1

Credits
Author: Shirley Pearson
Copy Editor: Karen Seberg

Visit carsondellosa.com for correlations to Common Core, state, national, and Canadian provincial standards.

Carson-Dellosa Publishing, LLC
PO Box 35665
Greensboro, NC 27425 USA
carsondellosa.com

ISBN 978-1-4838-1453-7
01-005151151

Table of Contents

Introduction

Common Core writing standards focus on three main text types: opinion/argumentative, informative/explanatory, and narrative. A fourth category, research writing, is essential to any evidence-based writing program.

Research shows that effective writing strategies include every step of the writing process: prewriting/brainstorming, drafting, revising, editing/proofreading, and publishing. Students will be walked through these steps on pages 6–10. The Writing Practice Packet can be reused for additional practice by changing the topic.

The writing exercises in this book are designed to go beyond basic writing conventions. Students will learn how to base opinions on evidence, infer facts from relevant details, convey accurate background information, and recount real or imagined experiences. Students' critical thinking skills are engaged when they do research, consider and analyze information, and respond to writing prompts. Writing prompts are paired with graphic organizers and followed by thinking/writing challenges.

Common Core Alignment Chart

Use this chart to plan instruction, practice, or remediation of a standard.

Common Core State Standards*		Practice Pages
Writing Standards		
Text Types and Purposes	1.W.1–1.W.3	11–63
Production and Distribution of Writing	1.W.5–1.W.6	11, 13, 17–36, 40, 42, 45–47, 50–63
Research to Build and Present Knowledge	1.W.7–1.W.8	11–63
Language Standards		
Conventions of Standard English	1.L.1–1.L.2	11–15, 18–29, 32–40, 42, 44–46, 49, 51–57, 59, 61–63
Vocabulary Acquisition and Use	1.L.4–1.L.6	11, 16, 17, 25, 30, 31, 41, 43, 47, 48, 50, 58, 60

*© Copyright 2010. National Governors Association Center for Best Practices and Council of Chief State School Officers. All rights reserved.

About This Book

Use this book to teach your students to read closely, or to notice words, structure, and points of fact. The writing prompts that begin on page 11 are intended to engage students' interests and then to send them off on a hunt for more information. Graphic organizers will help students organize their thoughts and research notes. Their actual writing will take place on separate sheets of paper. Encourage students to share their writing with peers, teachers, and other adults. Show students how to use the Student Writing Checklist on page 5. Allow time for thoughtful revisions. Publication is an important Common Core component of writing standards; students should be given access to computers, tablets, or copying machines.

Common Core-Aligned Writing Rubric

Use this rubric as a guide to assess students' written work. You may also offer it to students to help them check their work or as a tool to show your scoring.

4	_____ Offers insightful reasoning and strong evidence of critical thinking _____ Responds skillfully to all of the items in the prompt _____ Demonstrates a strong understanding of the text _____ Uses a logical organizational structure, including an introductory sentence, facts, and a concluding sentence _____ Skillfully supports topic(s) and opinions with evidence
3	_____ Offers sufficient reasoning and evidence of critical thinking _____ Responds to all items in the prompt _____ Demonstrates an understanding of the text _____ Uses an introductory and concluding sentence _____ Supports topic(s) and opinions with evidence
2	_____ Demonstrates some evidence of critical thinking _____ Responds to some items in the prompt _____ Demonstrates limited understanding of the text _____ Gives either an introductory or concluding sentence _____ Uses little evidence to support topic(s) and opinions
1	_____ Demonstrates limited or no evidence of critical thinking _____ Responds to some or no items in the prompts _____ Demonstrates little or no understanding of the text _____ Offers no introductory or concluding sentences _____ Uses no evidence to support topic(s) or opinions

Student Writing Checklist

Prewrite/Brainstorm

_____ Choose a topic.

_____ Look for your topic on the Internet, in books, or in magazines.

_____ Talk to other people about your topic.

_____ Gather facts.

_____ Take notes.

Draft

_____ Write a beginning, middle, and end.

_____ Tell why you think what you do.

_____ Use definitions and facts in your writing.

_____ Tell details about thoughts, feelings, or actions.

Revise

_____ Write each sentence with a subject and verb.

_____ Tell the story in the right order.

_____ Make sure sentence meaning is clear.

_____ Use specific nouns, exciting verbs, and interesting adjectives.

Edit/Proofread

_____ Capitalize the first letter in a sentence and all proper names.

_____ Use proper grammar, including subject/verb agreement.

_____ Use proper punctuation.

Publish

_____ Use your best handwriting or typing.

_____ Add picture(s) as needed.

Step 1: Prewrite/Brainstorm

Think about, plan, and organize your writing. Use the Internet, books, or magazines to find new information about your topic. Take notes.

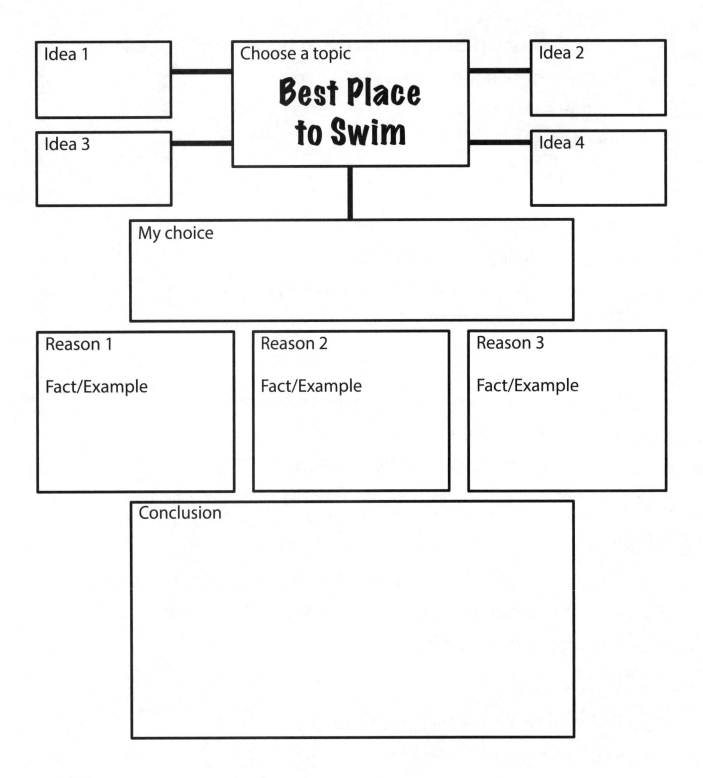

Idea 1

Idea 3

Choose a topic

Best Place to Swim

Idea 2

Idea 4

My choice

Reason 1

Fact/Example

Reason 2

Fact/Example

Reason 3

Fact/Example

Conclusion

Step 2: Draft

Use the notes from the organizer on page 6. Write a story about your topic. Remember to list reasons to support your opinion. Use linking words or phrases such as *because* and *for example*. In your ending sentence, restate your opinion.

_____

_____

_____

_____

_____

_____

_____

_____

_____

_____

_____

_____

_____

_____

Step 3: Revise

Read your story. Then, answer the questions with *Y* for *yes* or *N* for *no*.

_____ Did I start my story with an interesting introduction that will make readers want to read more?

_____ Did I list reasons to support my opinion?

_____ Did I use words such as *because* and *for example* to link my reasons with my opinion?

_____ Are all of my sentences about the topic?

_____ Should I add more details?

_____ Have I used exciting verbs?

_____ Have I used interesting adjectives?

_____ Does my conclusion provide a good ending for the story?

The best part of this story is	The part that needs work is

Step 4: Edit/Proofread

Place a check mark before each item when you have checked your work.

My Story

_____	I have read my story, and it makes sense.
_____	It has a beginning, middle, and end.
_____	I stayed on topic.
_____	My sentences are easy for readers to understand.
_____	I used a variety of words.

Capitalization

_____	Each sentence begins with a capital letter.
_____	All proper nouns begin with capital letters.

Punctuation

_____	Each sentence ends with the correct ending punctuation.
_____	I have placed commas where they belong.

Spelling

_____	I have checked to see that all words are spelled correctly.
_____	I have looked up words when needed.

Grammar

_____	My subjects and verbs match.
_____	I have used suffixes and prefixes properly.

Peer or Teacher Editing Checklist

Ask another student or teacher to look at your writing and mark *Yes* or *No*.

Is the first word of each sentence capitalized?	Yes	No
Are the proper nouns capitalized?	Yes	No
Does each sentence end with a punctuation mark?	Yes	No
Are the words spelled correctly?	Yes	No
Are the paragraphs indented?	Yes	No
Is the handwriting or typing easy to read?	Yes	No

Editor's Name_____

Step 5: Publish

When you publish a story, you make it possible for others to read it. Your readers might be teachers, students, or family members.

To publish an impressive story, choose from these options.

1. I choose to publish my writing by

_____ writing it in neat handwriting.

_____ typing it on a computer.

_____ typing it on a tablet.

_____ copying it on a copier.

2. If I use a cover page, it will include

_____ the title.

_____ the author's name.

_____ the illustrator's name.

_____ art or decoration.

3. If appropriate, my presentation will include

_____ illustration(s) or art.

_____ captions for the illustration(s).

_____ a graph, chart, or time line.

4. I will share my writing with

_____   _____

_____   _____

Name _____

Best Fit for Your Best Friend

People have pets for different reasons. Some want to ride horses. Some want to hug hamsters. Some want to look at fish. A pet must fit into a family. Dogs need to go outside. Cats can make you sneeze. Birds can be loud.

Ask your friends about their pets. What would be a good pet for you? Be sure to give reasons for your opinion.

Prewrite: Write your friends' responses in the organizer.

My Friends' Pets		
Pet 1	Pet 2	Pet 3
_____	_____	_____
Pros	Pros	Pros
_____ _____	_____ _____	_____ _____
Cons	Cons	Cons
_____ _____	_____ _____	_____ _____

☀ Reflect and Revise

1. Would your opinion change if the best pet for you were a snake? Explain your answer.

2. *Pet* can be used as a noun or a verb. Did you use the word *pet* both ways? Add another sentence if you did not.

Name _____

A Choice Spot

Do you ride a bus to school? Some students can choose their seats on the bus. Where would you like to sit? Would you sit at the back so that you can see everyone? Would you sit at the front to be close to the door? Talk to your friends. Where would they like to sit on the bus? Why?

Give reasons for your answer. Use prepositions of place such as *beside* and *in front*.

Prewrite: Write your friends' names in the organizer. Let them choose where to sit. Write your name too.

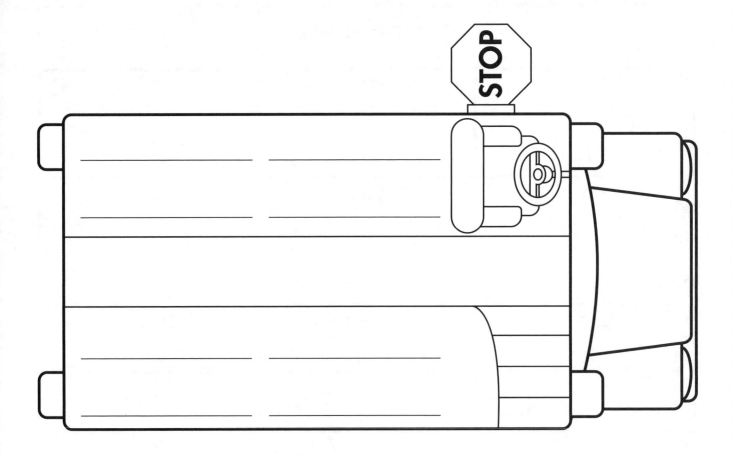

✺ Reflect and Revise

1. Choose another place to sit on the bus. Add a sentence to your story explaining your second choice.

2. Did you spell words correctly? Fix them if you did not.

Name _____

Sports Fan!

A cricket is not just an insect. It is also a sport! Cricket is a game like baseball. It is a team sport. You play with a bat and ball. You score runs to win. Cricket is a very popular sport.

There are many other fun sports to play. What is your favorite sport? Explain why it is your favorite. Use complete sentences.

Prewrite: List things about your favorite sport in the organizer.

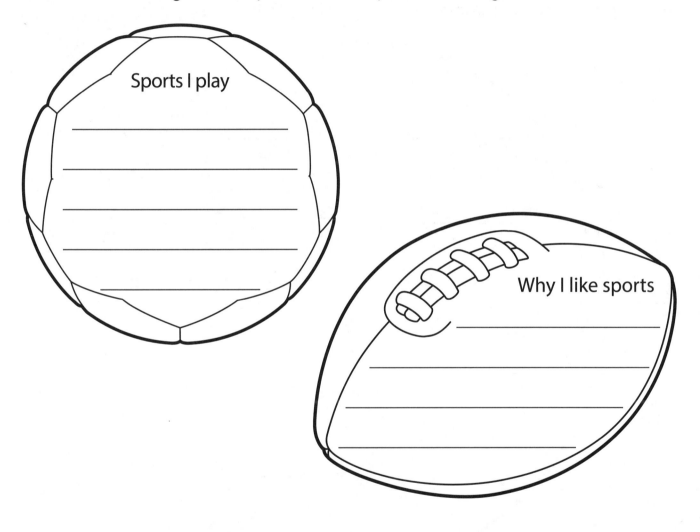

Sports I play

Why I like sports

My favorite sport is _____.

☀ Reflect and Revise

1. What sport would you *never* want to play? Why?

2. Did you use verbs correctly? Fix them if you did not.

Name _____

Big Parks

Playgrounds are small parks. National parks are big parks. Yellowstone is the oldest national park. It has many geysers. A geyser is a hole in the ground. It shoots up a fountain of hot water. Old Faithful is a famous geyser.

Ask adults about national parks they have visited. Read about national parks in a book or on the Internet. Which park would you like to visit? Give reasons for your answer.

Prewrite: Write some facts about national parks in the organizer.

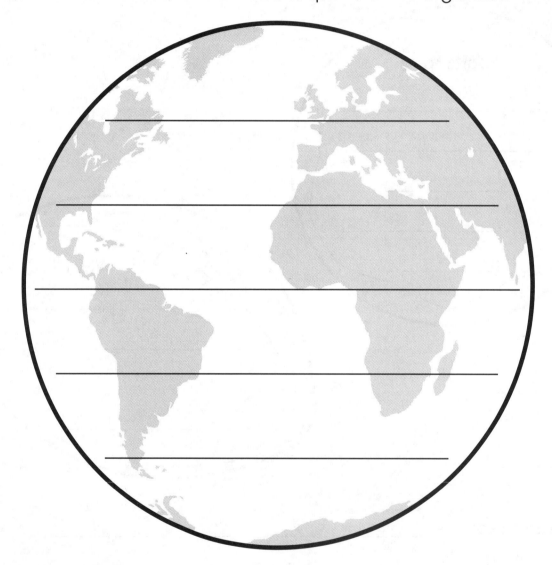

☀ Reflect and Revise

1. Think about a place you enjoy visiting. Should it become a national park? Explain your answer.

2. Did you use capital letters correctly? Fix them if you did not.

Name _____

My Number One Toy

Children have always played with toys. Toys can be simple. A stick can be a toy. Toys can be complicated. A video game is a toy. You can use toys to play games. They can be make-believe games. They can be real-life games. They can be sports games.

What kinds of toys do you like? Think about your favorite toy. Write your opinion. Give reasons why this toy is your favorite.

Prewrite: List three toys in the organizer. Write reasons you like these toys.

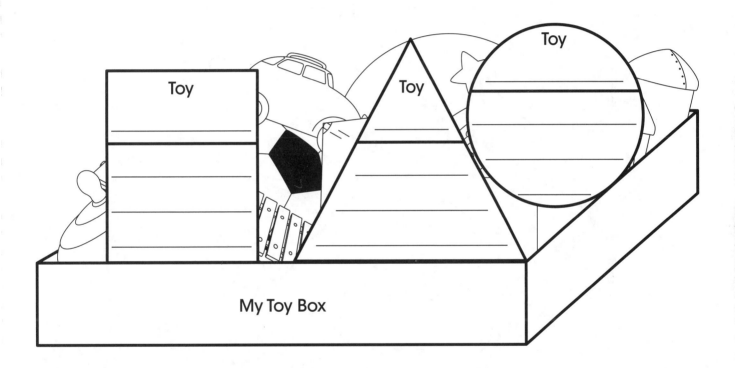

My favorite toy is _____ .

✺ Reflect and Revise

1. Do you have any toys that you never play with? Explain why.

2. Did you use possessive pronouns such as *my* or *their* correctly? Fix them if you did not.

Name _____

A Night under the Stars

Have you ever slept in a tent? If you have, you have been camping! Camping is living outdoors. Where you live is called your camp. Your house is a tent. Your stove is a fire. Your bed is a sleeping bag. The moon is your light.

Ask your friends if they have camped. Read about camping in a book or on the Internet. What are some things you like about camping? Give reasons for your opinion.

Prewrite: Fill in the organizer to tell what you know about camping.

When I camp, I like to...

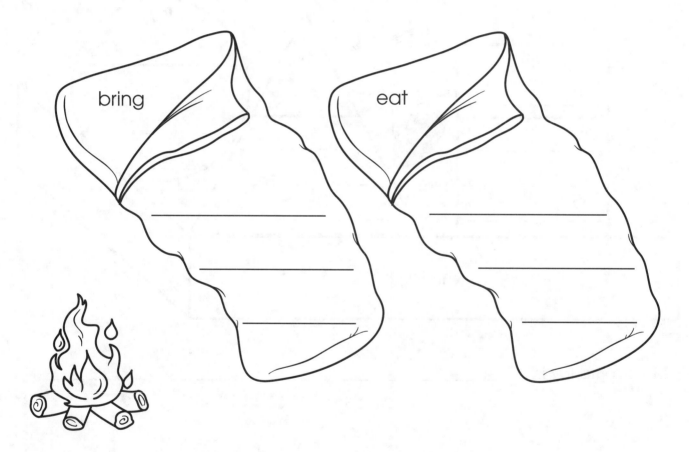

bring

eat

☀ Reflect and Revise

1. Some people camp in trailers. Other people camp without even a tent. Which do you think you would like better? Explain.

2. Add a sentence using a word that begins with *camp* and has an ending.

Name _____

Flower Power

Flowers are pretty. They grow in many colors. They grow in many sizes. They grow in many ways. Some flowers must be planted every year. Some grow back all by themselves! Flowers need rain and sunshine. Some need a little. Some need a lot.

What kinds of flowers do you like? Read about flowers in a book or on the Internet. What is your favorite flower? Give reasons for your opinion.

Prewrite: Fill in the organizer. Write the name of a flower you like on each line. Then, write why you like it.

Flower _____   Flower _____

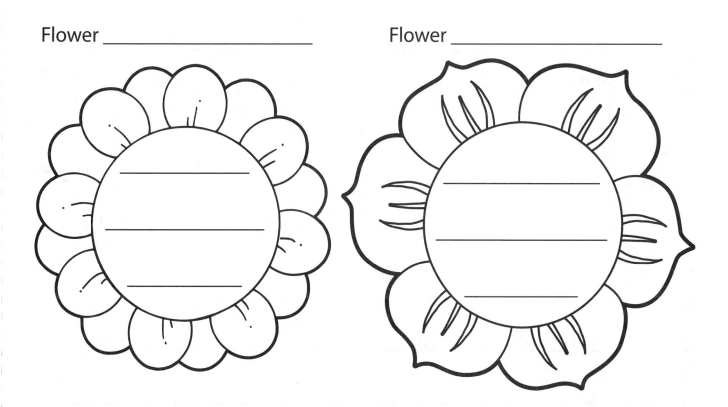

☀ Reflect and Revise

1. Pretend you live in a cloudy area. Will your favorite flower grow well there? Why or why not?

2. Did you use the correct adjectives to describe size? Fix them if you did not.

Name _____

We Want Your Vote!

The United States is a democracy. We choose our government. This choice is called a vote. We vote for many things. We vote for a person, such as the president. We vote for a thing, such as a swimming pool. We vote for an idea, such as clean air.

Choose a movie you want to see. Ask your friends to vote on it. Find out who else likes this movie. Do you think you and your friends should watch this movie? Write your opinion. Give reasons.

Prewrite: Fill in the organizer. Choose a topic to vote on. Put one mark under *YES* or *NO* for each person's vote. Remember to mark your own vote. Add up the total votes.

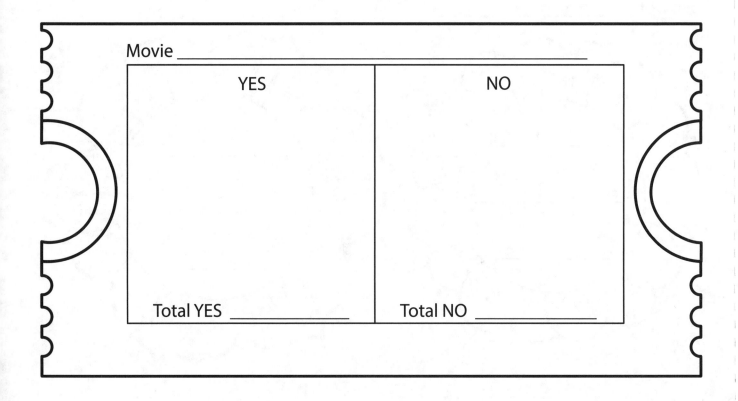

Movie _____

YES	NO
Total YES _____	Total NO _____

☀ Reflect and Revise

1. What should happen if the vote is tied? Explain your opinion.

2. Did you use conjunctions such as *and, but, or, so,* or *because* correctly? Fix them if you did not.

Name _____

Trees, Please!

Trees are more than just big plants. We use trees for many things. Oak trees give us wood. Apple trees give us fruit. Sassafras trees give us oil. Trees also give us things we cannot touch. They give us shady picnic spots. They give us fresh air.

What kinds of trees grow near you? Ask an adult about the trees you see. Read about trees in a book or on the Internet. Which tree do you think is the most useful? Write your opinion. Give reasons.

Prewrite: List three types of trees in the organizer. Write some things that these trees give us.

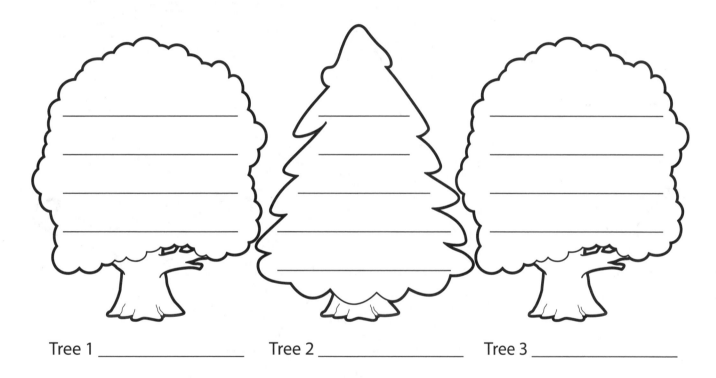

Tree 1 _____   Tree 2 _____   Tree 3 _____

I think the most useful tree is _____ .

☀ Reflect and Revise

1. Animals and insects use trees too. How? Add your answer to your essay.

2. Did you use ending punctuation marks correctly? Fix them if you did not.

Name _____

Eat Your Greens!

Do you eat vegetables? They are delicious! They are also good for you. Beets are beautiful and red. Carrots are crunchy and orange. Eggplant is exciting and purple. But, most vegetables are green. Dark green vegetables are very good for you.

Read about green vegetables in a book or on the Internet. Which two green vegetables do you like best? Explain why they are your favorites.

Prewrite: Write the names of some green vegetables in the organizer.

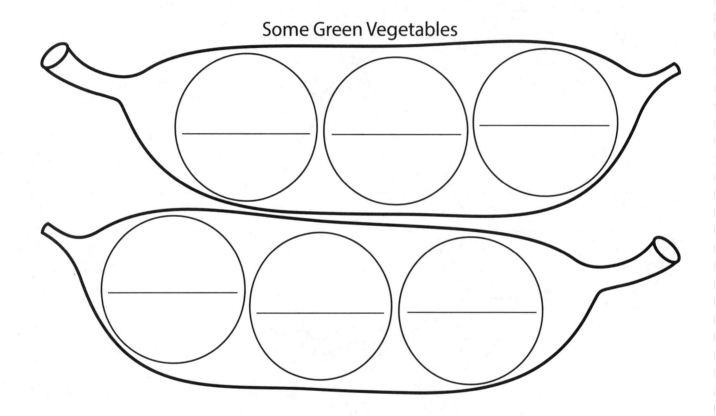

Some Green Vegetables

Two green vegetables that I like best are _____ and _____.

☀ Reflect and Revise

1. Think of some vegetables you do not like to eat. Is it because you do not like how they taste? Is it because you do not like how they look?

2. Did you use conjunctions such as *and*, *but*, *or*, *so*, or *because* correctly? Fix them if you did not.

Name _____

Treasured Books

A library is like a treasure chest. Books are like gold coins. They are precious. Most books have words. Some books have pictures. Books can tell stories. Books can give facts.

What is your favorite book? Write your opinion. Explain why you like this book.

Prewrite: Fill in the organizer with kinds of books you like to read. Then, write reasons why you like to read these books. Write the name of your favorite book.

I like to read

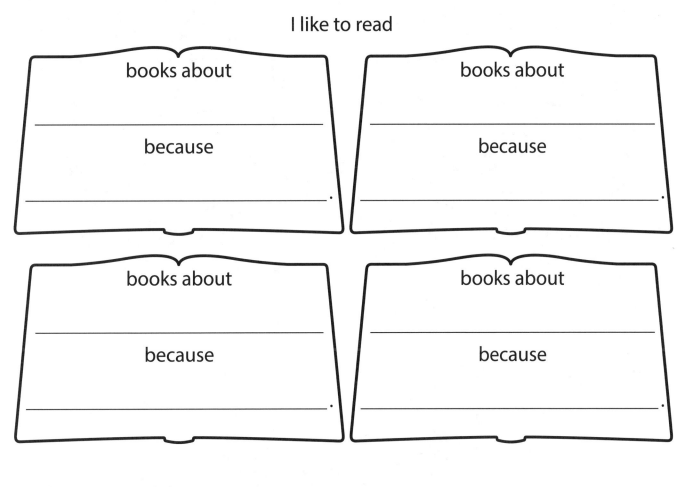

My favorite book is _____ .

⚡ Reflect and Revise

1. Do you like books with pictures? Why or why not? Explain.

2. Did you use capital letters correctly in the title of your book? Fix it if you did not.

Name _____

Pick a Party

Birthday parties are fun. Some parties are big. Some are small. Some parties are inside. Some are outside. Going to a party is fun. Having one is fun. What makes parties so great?

What is your favorite thing about birthday parties? Give reasons for your answer.

Prewrite: Fill in the organizer with party ideas.

People I like to be with

What I like to do

Things I like to eat

Reflect and Revise

1. What makes you feel special on your birthday? Why?

2. Add an exclamatory sentence to your writing.

Name _____

I Spy

Look around you. Look outside. What do you see? You see colors, lots of colors! We are luckier than our dogs. Dogs cannot see as many colors as we can.

What color do you think is most common? What color do you see most in things around you? Write your answer. Explain why you chose this color.

Prewrite: Play the I Spy game with friends. Look for colors. Fill in the organizer with things you see.

I Spy

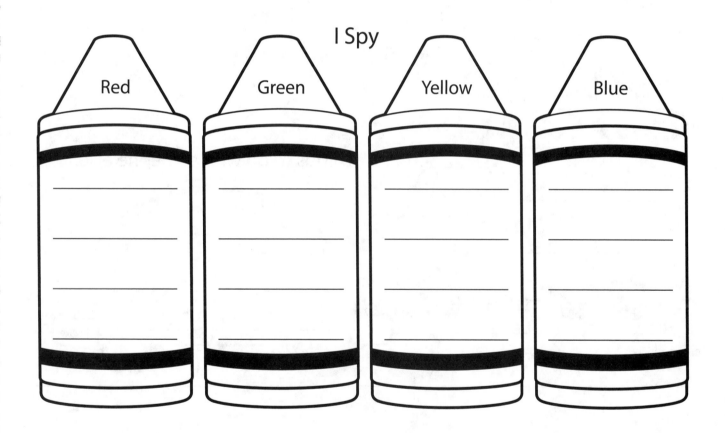

Red   Green   Yellow   Blue

✦ Reflect and Revise

1. What if you could only see in black and white? How would your life change? Explain.

2. Did you use conjunctions such as *and, but, or, so,* and *because* correctly? Fix them if you did not.

Name _____

On the Road

Have you ever been on a long trip? Did you go in a car? Did you go on a train? Did you go in an airplane? You are too young to drive! So, you are stuck in your seat.

It is more interesting to travel when you have things to do. In a car, you can count cows. You can play the alphabet game with signs. What else can you do? Look in books and magazines for ideas. Write about different things to do when you travel. Make sure you write an ending sentence.

Prewrite: Some travel games are fun to play alone. Some travel games can only be played with another person. Write travel game ideas on the lines.

Things to do by myself...

Things to do with someone else...

☀ Reflect and Revise

1. You wrote about things to do on a trip. How does your answer change if your trip is on a train or in an airplane? Explain.

2. Did you use verb tenses correctly to show time? Fix them if you did not.

Name _____

Dressed for Success

We do not have fur like bears. We do not have scales like fish. We do not have feathers like birds. We wear clothes instead. Clothes protect our bodies. We wear many types of clothes. Clothes cover different body parts.

Look in books and magazines to see what people wear in different places. Choose pieces of clothing to make an outfit. Draw a picture of yourself wearing the outfit. Then, write a description of your outfit. Use interesting adjectives.

Prewrite: List clothes in the organizer to choose from as you write. Group the clothes by body part.

Head	Chest	Legs	Feet

Reflect and Revise

1. Pretend you live where it is very cold. What clothes will you wear the most? Explain.

2. Did you use possessive pronouns such as *my* or *their* correctly? Fix them if you did not.

Tag! You Are It!

Tag is a fast game. You have to run a lot. Sometimes, you are running away. Sometimes, you are chasing. The person who is chasing is called it. How did you learn to play tag? Did someone tell you the rules? Did you watch other children play?

Explain the steps of playing tag. Use complete sentences.

Prewrite: How do you play tag? Write the steps in the organizer.

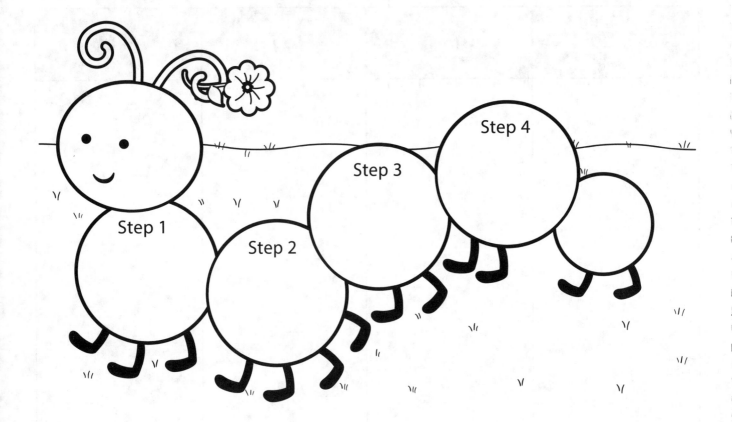

☀ Reflect and Revise

1. What is the best thing about being it when you play tag? What is the best thing about being chased? Are they the same? Explain.

2. Did you use verbs correctly? Fix them if you did not.

Name _____

Just Fix It

What do you do when something breaks? Do you throw it away? Do you try to fix it? There are many ways to fix things. Some things can be fixed in more than one way.

Think about how broken things are fixed. Choose a tool. What does it fix best? Why? Write your answer using complete sentences.

Prewrite: Look at the tools in the organizer. Write things they can fix.

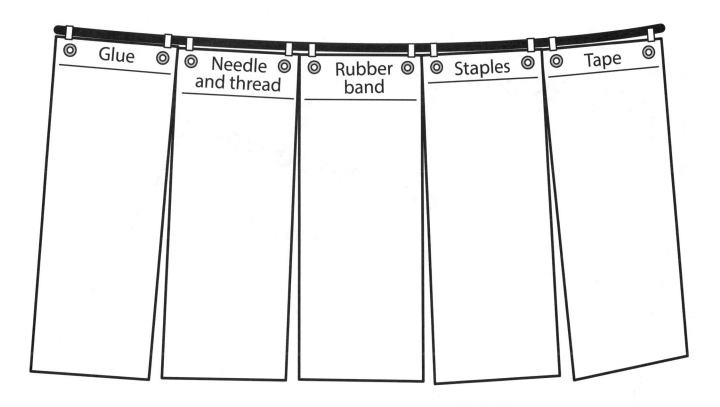

My favorite tool is the _____

because _____ .

☀ Reflect and Revise

1. Think about something you have helped to fix. Write the steps.

2. Did you use ending punctuation marks correctly? Fix them if you did not.

Playground Notes

Playgrounds are built for playing! You can play alone. You can play with a brother or sister. You can play with friends. Most playgrounds have things to play on, such as swings. Some playgrounds have ponds or fields nearby.

Think about playgrounds you have seen. Write about a playground you would like to play on. Use exciting verbs.

Prewrite: Use the organizer. Write about things you would like to play on at a playground.

I would like a

I would like a

✺ Reflect and Revise

1. Pretend your favorite playground was moved inside. Would the playground have to change? Why or why not?

2. Add an exclamatory sentence to your writing.

Name _____

Discover the Desert

There are deserts all over the world. The Sonoran Desert is in the United States. The Sahara Desert is in Africa. The Gobi Desert is in Asia. There is even a desert in Antarctica!

What do you know about deserts? Read about deserts in books or on the Internet. Then, write three sentences about deserts. Use interesting adjectives.

Prewrite: Use the organizer. Fill in the pyramids with words that describe deserts.

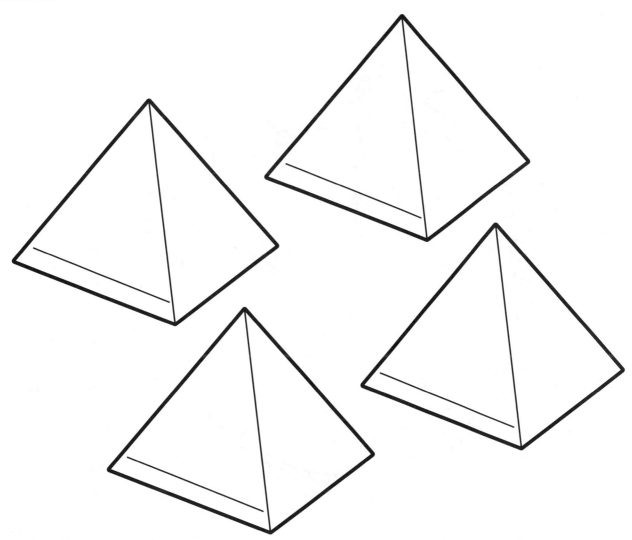

Reflect and Revise

1. Read about a cold desert such as the Gobi Desert. Does this change your idea of what a desert is like? Explain.

2. Did you capitalize all place names correctly? Fix them if you did not.

Round and Round

A wheel is part of a simple machine. A wheel is round. It rolls. It goes around its center. It is hard to imagine life without the wheel.

Look around your home. Look around your school. Look around your neighborhood. You will see a lot of wheels! Describe something with wheels. Use complete sentences.

Prewrite: Use the organizer. List five things you see that have wheels. Draw pictures of these things.

Things with wheels

☀ Reflect and Revise

1. What if there were no wheels? You would not ride a bus to school. What else would be different? Add a sentence to your report.

2. Add more interesting adjectives to your writing.

Name _____

Caring Communities

People care for people. Your family cares for you at home. Your teacher cares for you at school.

Think of people who live or work in your neighborhood. Think about what they do. Choose a worker who you know. Ask questions. Write how this person cares for you.

Prewrite: Pick four people whose jobs or actions show that they care. Use the organizer. Write notes about what these caring people do. Choose one for your writing.

A _____ cares.

A _____ cares.

A _____ cares.

A _____ cares.

Together we create a caring community.

 Reflect and Revise

1. Do you take care of anyone or anything? Who or what do you care for? Add a sentence to your essay to tell about the person or thing you take care of.

2. Add a sentence using a word that begins with *care* and has an ending.

Name _____

Castles in the Sand

You may not live in a castle. But, you can build one! You need sand. Water is good too. You need tools. A shovel is a tool. You need decorations. A shell is a decoration. Do you need help? Friends are great helpers.

Draw a picture of a sand castle. Be creative! Describe your castle in words. Use complete sentences.

Prewrite: Fill in the organizer with sand castle ideas.

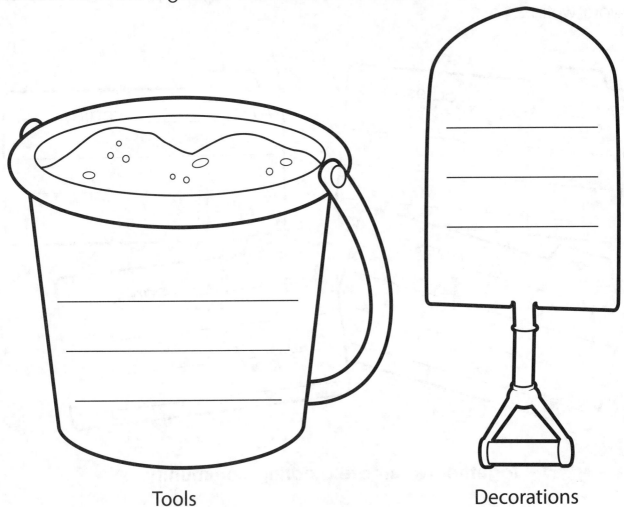

Tools   Decorations

☀ Reflect and Revise

1. There are many castles in the world. Some are hundreds of years old. Will your sand castle last that long? Why or why not?

2. Pretend you are building this castle tomorrow. What words will change in your story?

Name _____

Which Home for Me—the Farm or the Sea?

Some animals live on farms. These animals are not wild. They are domesticated. This means they are tame. We use farm animals for food. We use them for clothing. We use them for fun.

Many animals live in the sea. Some live near the top. This is where the water meets the air. Some live at the bottom. They never see the sun. Describe one farm animal and one sea animal.

Prewrite: Use the organizer. List some farm animals. List some sea animals.

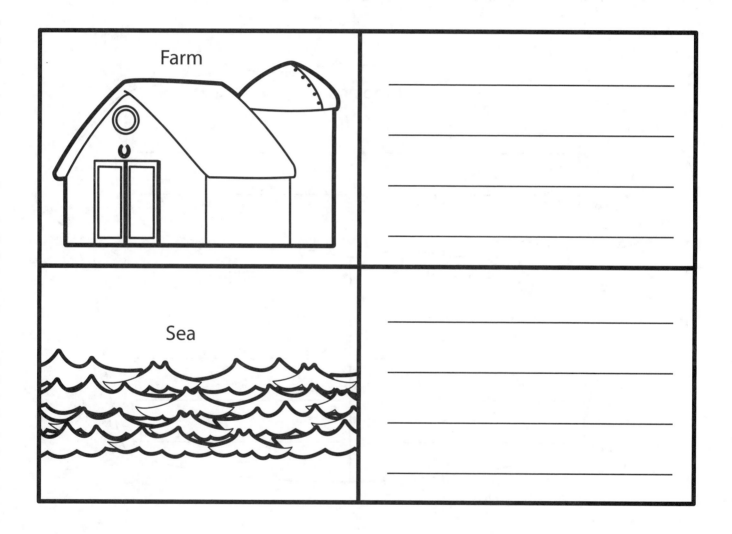

☀ Reflect and Revise

1. Some farmers raise fish. What do you think a fish farm looks like? Draw a picture. Then, read about fish farms in a book or on the Internet.

2. Did you use commas correctly? Fix them if you did not.

Name _____

Cupcake Party

Cupcakes are small cakes. They are baked in a cupcake pan. The pan has small molds to hold the cupcake batter. The molds are shaped like cups.

Not all cupcakes taste the same. They are baked with different flavors. Cupcakes are pretty. Some have fancy tops. Some have yummy fillings. Look at pictures of cupcakes in books, magazines, or on the Internet. Write about two very special cupcakes. Draw pictures of them.

Prewrite: Fill in the organizer with cupcake ideas.

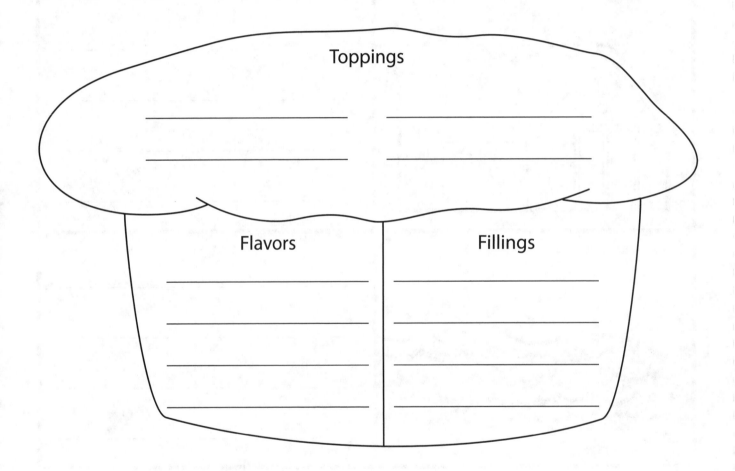

Toppings

_____   _____

_____   _____

Flavors   Fillings

_____   _____

_____   _____

_____   _____

_____   _____

Reflect and Revise

1. Explain why you might want to make cupcakes instead of one big cake.

2. Add a question to the beginning of your report.

Name _____

Shopping Trip

Think about a time you were in a store. What kind of store was it? Did you buy anything?

People buy things for different reasons. Sometimes, they need things. Sometimes, they want things. Think of all of the things stores sell! What things do you and your family buy? Look at catalogs or store coupons for more ideas. Then, write about a shopping trip you would like to take.

Prewrite: Fill in the organizer with things stores sell.

Things to eat	Things to wear	Things to play with

✸ Reflect and Revise

1. What things do you both need and want? Explain why.

2. Did you use conjunctions such as *and*, *but*, *or*, *so*, or *because*? Add them if you did not.

Buggy Pests

Do flies bug you? Is an ant a pest? Do you want a spider in your bed? Flies, ants, and spiders are bugs. Bugs with six legs are called insects. Bugs are creepy, crawly things. Bugs are pests. Sometimes, they are good pests.

Read about bugs in a book or on the Internet. Are some bugs helpful? How do they help? Write a report about helpful bugs.

Prewrite: Draw pictures of four helpful bugs in the organizer.

Bug 1 _____	Bug 2 _____
Bug 3 _____	Bug 4 _____

☼ Reflect and Revise

1. What would happen if there were no bugs? Explain.

2. Did you spell words correctly? Fix them if you did not.

Fish Tales

Many people fish. Some people eat the fish they catch. Some people sell the fish. Some people throw them back! There are many ways to fish. Some boats have big nets. The nets pull in a lot of fish at one time. Some boats have fishing rods. The rods are very strong. They can even reel in a shark!

Imagine you are going fishing. Write a story about your fishing trip. Be descriptive.

Prewrite: Use the organizer to plan your trip. Answer the questions.

My Fishing Trip	
Who? Am I alone? Am I with a friend?	
What? Am I fishing from a boat, a dock, or the shore?	
Where? Am I at a pond, a lake, or an ocean?	
When? Is it summer, Saturday, or morning?	
Why? Do I want to eat the fish? Am I fishing for another reason?	
How? Am I using a net, a rod, a hook, or a pail?	

Reflect and Revise

1. Imagine fishing is your job. You live on your boat. You even fish when it rains. Rewrite your story.

2. Did you use commas correctly? Fix them if you did not.

Name _____

Take Me to the Fair!

Raul is excited. The fair is in town. Raul loves the fair! His mother is taking Raul and his little brother. It is a special family treat. They are going next week. Megan is Raul's best friend. Megan is excited about the fair too. Her family is going tomorrow. Megan asks Raul to come. If Raul goes with Megan, his family will be sad. If he goes with his family, Megan will be sad. Raul's choice affects other people.

Think about a time when you had to make a choice like Raul must. Write a story about it. Use complete sentences.

Prewrite: Write about your choices in the organizer.

Choice 1

Choice 2   Choice 3

☀ Reflect and Revise

1. How did choice 1 make you feel? How did choice 2 make you feel? How about choice 3? Are these feelings the same?

2. Did you use conjunctions such as *and, but, or, so,* or *because*? Add them if you did not.

All by Myself

The passenger pigeon is extinct. The last one died in 1914. But, your grandfather's grandfather might have seen thousands of them! Passenger pigeons flew in huge flocks. The flocks were so big they blocked the sun. They filled trees with nests. There were so many that people thought they were pests. Now, there are none.

Pretend the year is 1900. You are a passenger pigeon. What is your life like? Write a story about it.

Prewrite: Use the organizer. Write your ideas on the eggs.

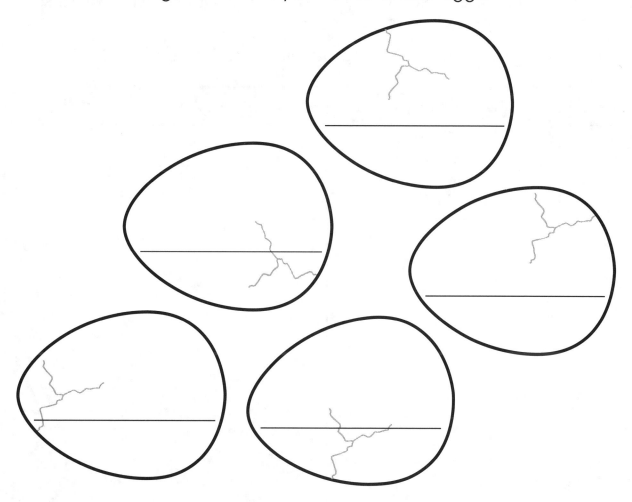

☀ Reflect and Revise

1. People did not realize passenger pigeons were becoming extinct. How could these birds have been saved?

2. Did you use the words *I, me,* and *my* in your story? Did you write as if you were a passenger pigeon? Fix your story if you did not.

The Tale of the Tailbone

Touch the back of your neck. Feel your backbone. That is your spine. It runs all of the way down to your tailbone. Animals with spines have tailbones. Many have tails too! Some animals have special tails. They can use their tails like hands. They can hold onto things with their tails. Spider monkeys have these tails. So do sea horses!

Look at pictures of animals with tails. Read what they do with their tails. Then, imagine you woke up with a tail! Write a story about how this would change some of the things you do. What could you do that you cannot do now? What is something you could no longer do? Make sure your story has a beginning and an end.

Prewrite: Write ideas about waking up with a tail in the organizer.

Why I would **like** having a tail	Why I would **not like** having a tail

☀ Reflect and Revise

1. What would be the best thing about having a tail? What would be the worst thing? Why?

2. Add an exclamatory sentence to your story.

Whatever the Weather

Look outside! What is the weather? Is it sunny? Is it cloudy? Is it windy? Weather can be extreme. Dry days can become droughts. Plants die. Rainstorms can become hurricanes. Streets flood. Thunderstorms can become tornadoes. Trees blow down.

Pretend you are on a picnic. Check the weather on TV or the Internet. What is it like now? Is it going to change? Write a story about how the weather can affect your picnic.

Prewrite: Use the organizer. Add words for a sunny day. Add words for a stormy day. Use the words in your story.

Sunny Words

Stormy Words

☀ Reflect and Revise

1. When do you need to know what the weather will be? How might the weather affect your plans? Explain your answer.

2. Did you spell words correctly? Fix them if you did not.

The Earth beneath Our Feet

Earth's crust is broken into pieces. These are slabs of rock. The slabs are called plates. The plates move. Sometimes, they slide against each other. Sometimes, they pull apart. This can cause an earthquake. Earthquakes are scary. Buildings fall down. Roads split open. Underwater earthquakes cause huge waves. Towns are flooded.

Read about earthquakes. Try to talk to someone who has been in one. Then, imagine you are in an earthquake. What do you see? Hear? Smell? Taste? Touch? What do you do? Write a story about being in an earthquake.

Prewrite: Fill in the organizer with your ideas.

See	Hear	Smell	Taste	Touch	Do

☀ Reflect and Revise

1. Earthquakes cause a lot of damage. How might we make buildings and people safer?

2. Did you use capital letters correctly? Fix them if you did not.

May I Borrow That, Please?

The Borrowers stories were written by Mary Norton. Borrowers are small people. They are shorter than pencils. Borrowers live in people's houses. They do not like to be seen. They borrow things. They use things that do not belong to them.

Read The Borrowers stories if you do not know them. Your teacher can help you find the books. Then, pretend you are a Borrower. Tell about something you borrowed and what you used it for.

Prewrite: Use the organizer. List some things you use. Then, write what a Borrower might use those things for.

Some things I use . . .	. . . can be used by a Borrower for something else!
bottle cap	frying pan

☀ Reflect and Revise

1. What are some things you could do better if you were very small? What are some things you would have trouble doing?

2. Add a sentence using a word that begins with *borrow* and has an ending.

A Dandelion Adventure

Dandelions are weeds. The yellow flowers die. Then, the dandelions turn white. These are the seed heads. Dandelion seeds are tiny. They float. Blow on them. They will fly away! When they land, they can grow into more dandelions.

Have you ever held a dandelion? Did you blow its seeds away? Try to remember. Pretend you are a dandelion seed. Write a story about your adventure. End your story when you find a new home.

Prewrite: Use the organizer. Answer the questions about your trip as a dandelion seed.

What blows on me?	What do I see when I fly?	How do I feel when I fly?	Where do I land?

Reflect and Revise

1. Dandelion leaves have jagged edges. *Dandelion* means lion's teeth in French. Is that a good name for this plant? Explain.

2. Did you use verb tenses correctly to show time? Fix them if you did not.

Name _____

Kite Fright

Benjamin Franklin is known for many things. His kite experiment is one of them. No one knew what lightning was. Franklin thought it was electricity. He wanted to be sure. One story says Franklin tied some metal wire to a kite. Then, he flew the kite in a storm! This was not a safe thing to do. Lightning hit the metal wire. It ran down the kite's string. It made an electric spark. Franklin's experiment worked!

Read more stories about this experiment. Then, pretend you are holding Franklin's kite. Imagine a storm has come up. Write a story about what happens next.

Prewrite: Use the organizer. Write words to describe the storm. Write words to describe your feelings.

The Storm   How I Feel

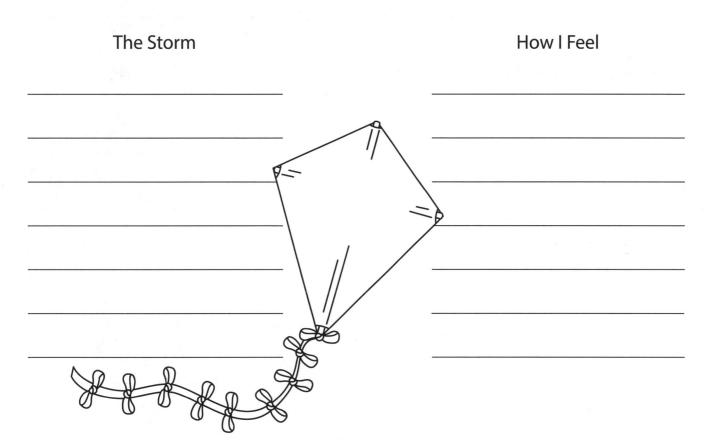

☀ Reflect and Revise

1. Benjamin Franklin knew his experiment was dangerous. Why do you think he did it?

2. Did you capitalize all proper names correctly? Fix them if you did not.

Name _____

River Run

Many rivers start in the mountains. The water is cold. The river is small. It meets other rivers. It grows bigger. Many rivers flow into the sea. Rivers do not flow in straight lines. They can be blocked by fallen trees. Some rivers are shallow. You can walk across them. Some are narrow. You can jump across them. The water can be rough and choppy. It can be calm and smooth.

Look at pictures of rivers in magazines or on the Internet. Imagine you are in a boat on a river. The river goes through many changes. Write a story about your trip.

Prewrite: Read the changes to the river. These are the *causes*. Write how this affects you and your trip. These are the *effects*.

Cause	Effect
Changes to the river	**How this affects me and my trip**
cold water	
narrow river	
joins other rivers	
fast water	
rough water	
shallow river	

☀ Reflect and Revise

1. Long ago, many people traveled by river. Why? Would you like to travel that way?

2. Add an exclamatory sentence to your story.

Name _____

Snow Day!

Have you ever had a snow day? A storm day? A heat day? These are days when school is closed. You wake up. You get ready for school. But, you do not have to go!

What would you do on a day with no school? What would your friends do? Ask them. Write a story about your day off from school. Use exciting verbs.

Prewrite: Write some fun ideas in the organizer. Pick one of them for your story.

What to do on a snow day	What to do on a storm day	What to do on a heat day
O _____ _____	O _____ _____	O _____ _____
O _____ _____	O _____ _____	O _____ _____
O _____ _____	O _____ _____	O _____ _____
O _____ _____	O _____ _____	O _____ _____

☀ Reflect and Revise

1. Did you ever stay home from school because you were sick? Compare that day off to a snow day.

2. Add more interesting adjectives to your story.

Name _____

Meet the President

Some countries have presidents. The United States has a president. The first US president was George Washington. The president is very important. The president lives in the White House. The White House is in Washington, D.C.

Imagine you will visit the president. You can bring anything you want. Do you bring your favorite toy? Do you bring your best friend? Write a story about your visit.

Prewrite: Fill in the organizer with your ideas.

What I Bring	What We Talk About	What We Do
_____	_____	_____
_____	_____	_____
_____	_____	_____
_____	_____	_____
_____	_____	_____

How I Feel _____

_____

Reflect and Revise

1. Would you like to be president some day? Why or why not?

2. Add more exciting verbs to your story.

Name _____

Where Am I Going?

In a popular story, a girl named Lucy finds a secret passage. It is like a tunnel. It goes to a new world. The world is called Narnia. Talking animals live there. One talking animal is a lion named Aslan. He is wise and kind.

Imagine you find a secret passage. Where does your secret passage start? Where does it go? Will you take someone along to explore with you? What do you see along the way? Is it going to be hard for you to get back home? Write a story about your adventure.

Prewrite: Answer the questions in the organizer.

Where does the passage start? _____	Where does the passage go? _____	What do I find?
_____	_____	_____
_____	_____	_____
		_____
How do I get home? _____	Whom do I meet? _____	_____
_____	_____	_____
_____	_____	

☀ Reflect and Revise

1. Would you tell your friends about your secret? Why or why not?

2. Add an exclamatory sentence to your story.

Name _____

Making Music

Instruments make music. A drum makes music. A horn makes music. A guitar makes music too. A xylophone is a simple instrument. It is made of bars. You hit the bars with a mallet. Each bar is a different length. Each bar sounds a different note. This creates music.

Read about an instrument in a book or on the Internet. Then, describe how this instrument works. Use complete sentences.

Prewrite: Fill in the organizer with facts about the instrument.

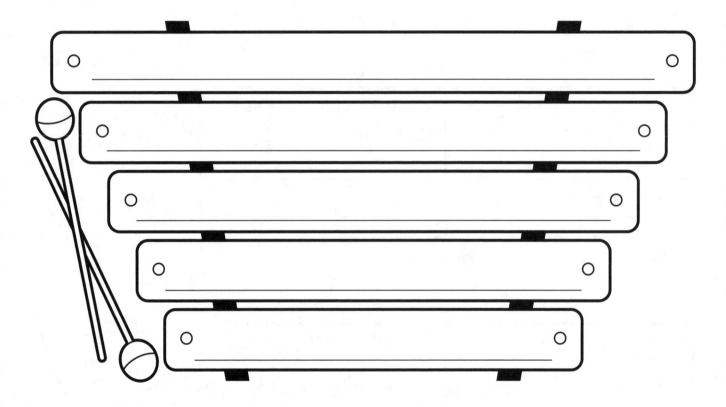

The instrument that interests me is a _____ .

 Reflect and Revise

1. Music can be quiet and soothing. Music can be loud and exciting. Which do you like better? Can the instrument you chose be played both ways?

2. Look at your verbs. Replace some with more interesting verbs that mean the same thing.

Name _____

Earth Is Not Alone

Earth is part of a solar system. The sun is at the center. Earth revolves around the sun. Other planets do too. The path each planet makes is an orbit.

Read about our solar system in a book or on the Internet. Write a description of Earth and another planet. Compare them.

Prewrite: Use the organizer. Write facts about Earth and another planet. Use the facts in your writing.

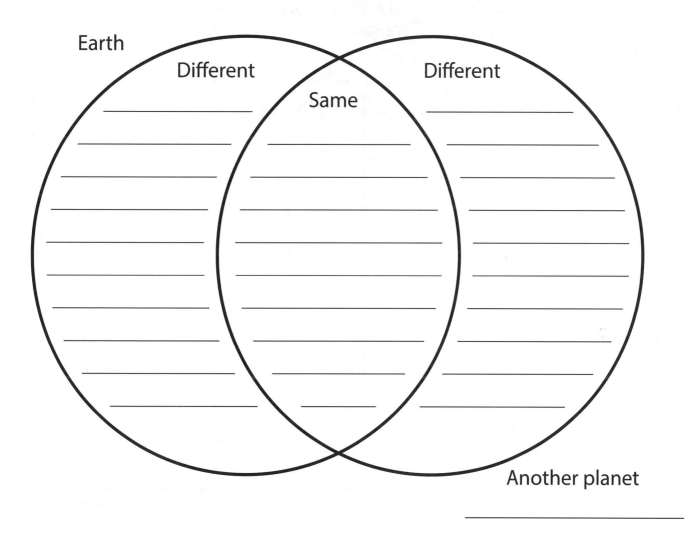

Earth

Different

Same

Different

Another planet

_____

☀ Reflect and Revise

1. Do you think humans could live on Earth if it were closer to the sun? What if Earth were farther from the sun? Explain your answer.

2. Did you use capital letters correctly? Fix them if you did not.

Fly Your Flag High

Each country has its own flag. Some flags are very simple. Some have fancy shapes. Some have many colors. Look at the flag of the United States. There are 13 stripes. These are for the 13 original colonies. There are 50 stars. These are for the 50 states.

Find a picture of the flag of your state, province, or country. Look in a book or on the Internet. Imagine a flag that stands for you. What would it look like? Describe your flag. Give reasons for your design.

Prewrite: Use the organizer. Draw the flag of your state, province, or country. Then, draw a flag that represents you. Use shapes, colors, and symbols.

The Flag of _____	The Flag of Me

☀ Reflect and Revise

1. Kiribati is a tiny country. Its flag has blue and white wavy lines. Look up Kiribati in an atlas or on the Internet. What do you think the wavy lines mean?

2. Did you use conjunctions such as *and, but, or, so,* or *because*? Add them if you did not.

Caterpillar Mystery

Have you ever seen a caterpillar? It looks a little bit like a short, fat worm. It has legs. It also has a secret! Caterpillars are babies. When they grow up, they change. They turn into insects. They fly! Some caterpillars become butterflies. Some become moths.

Read about these insects in a book or on the Internet. Then, write a report about them.

Prewrite: Use the organizer. Write some facts about moths and butterflies to use in your report.

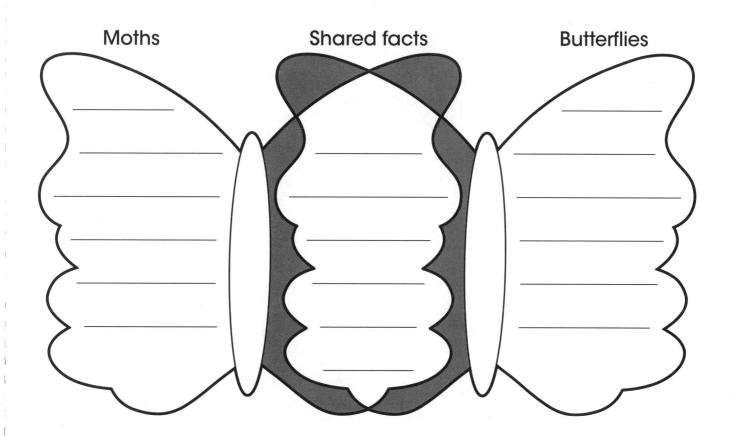

Moths   Shared facts   Butterflies

☀ Reflect and Revise

1. Pretend you could change into something else when you grow up. What would you change into? Why?

2. Add a question to the beginning of your report.

Wise Old Owl

All owls have large eyes. People think their large eyes make owls look wise. An owl can see very well with its eyes. But, an owl can only look forward. Owls' eyes do not move. How does an owl look away? It must move its head.

Read about owls in a book or on the Internet. There are many different kinds of owls. Write a report about one kind of owl.

Prewrite: Use the organizer to fill in facts about different owls. Choose one to write your report about.

Owl 1   Owl 2   Owl 3

Facts

Color

Size

Food

Nest

☀ Reflect and Revise

1. Owls can see in the dark much better than we can. Why is this important for owls?

2. Did you use commas correctly? Fix them if you did not.

Bizarre Beaks

er. Bees
o eat
hey wear

does a

the

hey have beaks. Birds use their beaks to take
at the shape of a bird's beak. The shape tells
d. The shape tells us what the bird eats!

book or on the Internet. Pick one bird that
hat cannot fly. Pick one bird that nests near
eaks different from each other? Write a report

with facts about bird beaks.

Trees	Cannot Fly	Nests near Water

xplain

vords in

of birds' feet. What do their different shapes

ectly? Fix them if you did not.

Name _____

Busy Bees

Have you ever watched a bee? A bee flies from flower to flo
gather nectar to make honey. Some people raise bees. They like
sweet, fresh honey. Bees can sting. Beekeepers must be careful.
special clothes. They use special tools.

Read about beekeeping in a book or on the Internet. What
beekeeper do? Describe a beekeeper's job.

Prewrite: Write some facts about beekeeping in the organizer. U
facts in your report.

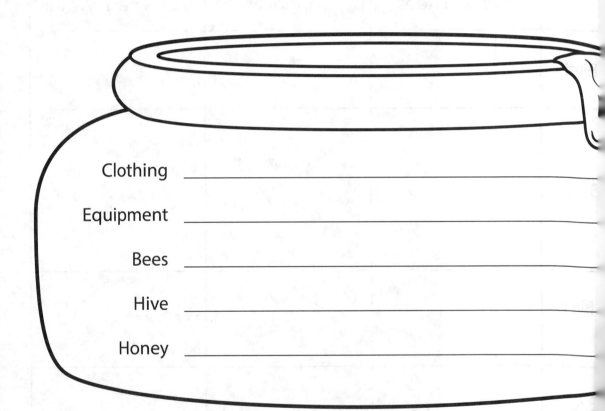

Clothing _____

Equipment _____

Bees _____

Hive _____

Honey _____

Reflect and Revise

1. Why do you think someone might become a beekeeper?
   your answer.

2. What if your report is about beekeeping in the past? What
   your report will change?

Name _____

A Little Bit of Ice

Have you heard of the *Titanic*? It was a huge ship. The *Titanic* was built to sail across the Atlantic Ocean. Its first trip was in 1912. People got on the ship in England. Many did not reach New York. The *Titanic* hit an iceberg. It was night. The iceberg was hard to see. The ship was far from land. It sank in less than three hours.

Read about icebergs in a book or on the Internet. Then, write what you have learned. Use complete sentences.

Prewrite: Answer the questions about icebergs in the organizer. Use the answers to help you write your report.

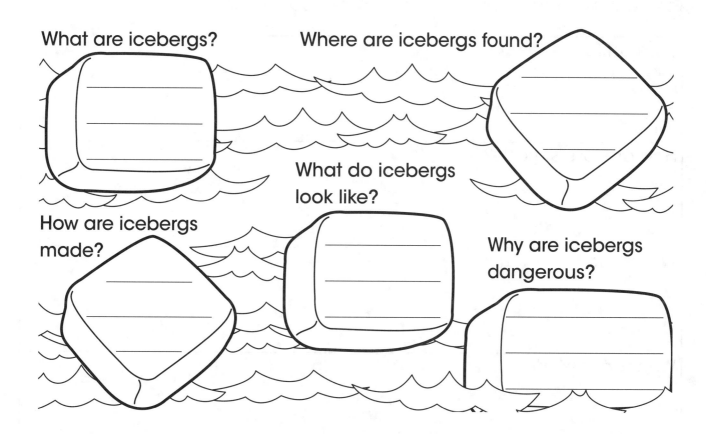

What are icebergs?

Where are icebergs found?

What do icebergs look like?

How are icebergs made?

Why are icebergs dangerous?

☀ Reflect and Revise

1. Earth is getting warmer. Ice is melting faster. Do you think this will affect icebergs? Explain your answer.

2. Do your singular and plural nouns and verbs match? Fix them if they do not.

Name _____

Fossil Secrets

We know what dogs look like because we can see them. We can read about dodo birds. We can see cave pictures of woolly mammoths. What about dinosaurs? That is not so easy.

Dinosaurs lived before humans. They left fossils. The word *fossil* comes from a Latin word that means dug up. We have to dig for most fossils. They tell us things. They tell us size. They tell us shape. They tell us about many plants and animals. Read about fossils in a book or on the Internet. Write four sentences about fossils.

Prewrite: Use the organizer to write facts about fossils.

Types of fossils
How are fossils made?
Where are fossils found?
What do fossils tell us?

☀ Reflect and Revise

1. Do you think it is important to know about things that lived long ago? Why or why not?

2. Add more interesting adjectives to your sentences.

Hidden City

Mexico City is the capital of Mexico. It is a big city. Under it is another city. This is a ruined city. It was the center of the Aztec empire. The Aztecs once ruled Mexico. They left many things behind. The Aztecs left their city. They left their food. They even left their language. The word *chocolate* comes from the Aztec language.

Read about the Aztecs in a book or on the Internet. Describe how the Aztecs lived.

Prewrite: Fill in the organizer with Aztec facts.

House Facts	Food Facts

Farm Facts	Clothing Facts

What do you think is the most interesting fact about the Aztecs?

☀ Reflect and Revise

1. Would you have liked to live with the Aztecs? Why or why not?

2. Did you use verb tenses correctly to show time? Fix them if you did not.

Name _____

Ice Cream

Where does ice cream come from? Does it come from the ice cream truck, the dairy bar, or the grocery store? Maybe ice cream comes from all three! Ice cream is very easy to eat. It slips down your throat. It is easy to make too. You just need an ice-cream machine. But, making ice cream was not always easy. Ice cream used to be made by hand.

Read about making ice cream in a book or on the Internet. Then, write a report about how to make ice cream.

Prewrite: Fill in the organizer with ice cream facts.

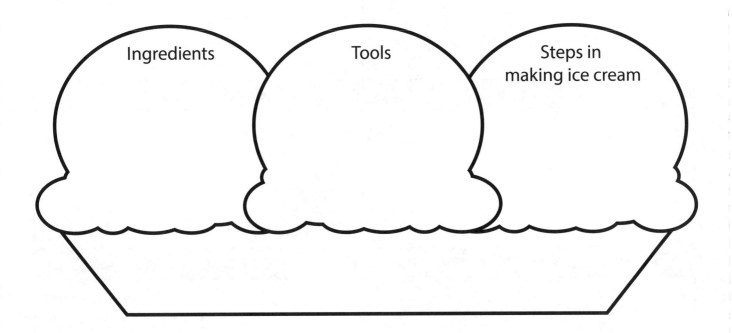

Ingredients

Tools

Steps in making ice cream

☀ Reflect and Revise

1. What do you think is the hardest part about making ice cream? Why?

2. Add more interesting adjectives to your report.

Name _____

Funny Feet

Cows have hoofs. Cats have paws. Hoofs are hard. Paws are spongy. Both are special kinds of feet.

Read about different animals. How do hoofs help some animals? How do paws help other animals? Why are hoofs and paws useful? Write your answer in complete sentences.

Prewrite: Fill in the organizer with some animal names.

Animals with Hoofs	Animals with Paws

Reflect and Revise

1. Do you think the life of a mountain goat would be different if goats had paws instead of hoofs? Explain.

2. Do your singular and plural nouns and verbs match? Fix them if they do not.

Name _____

A Long Way Home

   Geese migrate. They have two homes. One is for summer. This home is in the north. One is for winter. This home is in the south. Many animals migrate.

   Read about animals that migrate. Then, write about one of these animals. Explain why the animal migrates.

Prewrite: Fill in the organizer with facts about migrating animals.

Animal	Winter Home	Summer Home

☀ Reflect and Revise

1. Some geese live in the city. They do not migrate. Why do you think this is?

2. Did you capitalize all place names correctly? Fix them if you did not.

Hiding from Sight

Animals escape predators in different ways. Some animals run fast. Some animals hide in caves or trees. There are other ways to hide. Many animals look like the land around them. They blend in. This is called *camouflage*.

Read about animals in a book or on the Internet. Which animals hide by blending in? How do they blend in? Describe two animals that use camouflage.

Prewrite: List some animals that use camouflage in the organizer. List the kind of camouflage they use.

Animal	Camouflage

☀ Reflect and Revise

1. Think of an animal that does not use camouflage. Why do you think it does not?

2. Did you spell words correctly? Fix them if you did not.

Answer Key

Because writing is personal and presentations are unique, there are no "correct answers" to be applied to students' work. However, students should follow the instruction of the writing prompts, fill in the graphic organizers, and apply the steps of the writing process. Use the guidelines below or the Writing Rubric on page 4 to help you assess students' work.

Pages 6 to 10: Writing Practice Packet

Check students' work throughout the writing process practice pages. Help students master each step before going on to the next step. This process can be used with other writing prompts if more practice is needed before independent writing can begin. Refer students back to specific practice pages as needed.

Pages 11 to 63: Reflect and Revise

The Reflect and Revise section at the end of each writing prompt page asks students first to consider an alternative or additional slant to their topic. Often they are requested to add this additional layer of thought to their writing. Check that they have fulfilled the challenge and that their conclusions have been applied to the writing if asked. Because the Common Core language standards are tied so tightly to the writing standards, the second part addresses specific language skills. Check through written work for mastery.

Pages 11 to 23: Opinion/Argumentative Writing

Check graphic organizers. Writing will vary, but opinions should be supported with reasons and show evidence based on research, interviews, or recollection of experiences. Look for application of critical thinking and personal reflection.

Pages 24 to 36: Informative/Explanatory Writing

Check graphic organizers. Writing will vary but should be based on research or interviews. Look for facts rather than opinions. Information should be presented using the structure of an introduction, body, and conclusion. Facts should be grouped in paragraphs according to subtopic. Ideas should be connected with linking words and phrases.

Pages 37 to 49: Narrative Writing

Check graphic organizers. Stories, essays, and other narrative formats will vary but should respond to all of the items in the prompt. Look for clear and logical sequences of events using a variety of transitional words and phrases. Stories should include characters and setting as well as problems and solutions.

Pages 50 to 63: Research Writing

Check graphic organizers. Reports will vary but should be based on research or interviews. Assess students' abilities to examine topics and convey ideas and information clearly to their readers. Students should use logical organizational structures, including introductory and concluding sentences or paragraphs.